Math Basics

Penguin Patterns

By Nick Rebman

T0011636

level 1
little blue readers

www.littlebluehousebooks.com

Little Blue House is distributed by North Star Editions:
sales@northstareditions.com | 888-417-0195

Produced for Little Blue House by Red Line Editorial.

Photographs ©: Shutterstock Images, cover, 4–5, 6–7 (blue), 6–7 (red), 8–9 (penguin with hat), 8–9 (penguin), 8–9 (ties), 10–11 (real penguins), 12–13, 14–15 (red), 14–15 (green), 16 (top left), 16 (top right), 16 (bottom left), 16 (bottom right); iStockphoto, 10–11 (toys)

Library of Congress Control Number: 2020900832

ISBN
978-1-64619-168-0 (hardcover)
978-1-64619-202-1 (paperback)
978-1-64619-270-0 (ebook pdf)
978-1-64619-236-6 (hosted ebook)

Printed in the United States of America
Mankato, MN
012021

About the Author

Nick Rebman enjoys reading, walking his dog, and traveling to places where he doesn't speak the language. He lives in Minnesota.

Table of Contents

Penguin Patterns

A pattern is something that happens over and over.

penguin

tree

tree

One penguin is blue.

One penguin is red.

The pattern happens over and over.

One penguin has a hat.

One penguin has a tie.

The pattern happens over and over.

Two penguins are toys.

One penguin is real.

The pattern happens over and over.

Two penguins are small.

One penguin is big.

The pattern happens over and over.

One penguin is red.

Two penguins are green.

red

green

green

The pattern happens over and over.

red

green

green

Glossary

hat

tie

pattern

toy

Index